WHERE'S THE ZOMBIE?

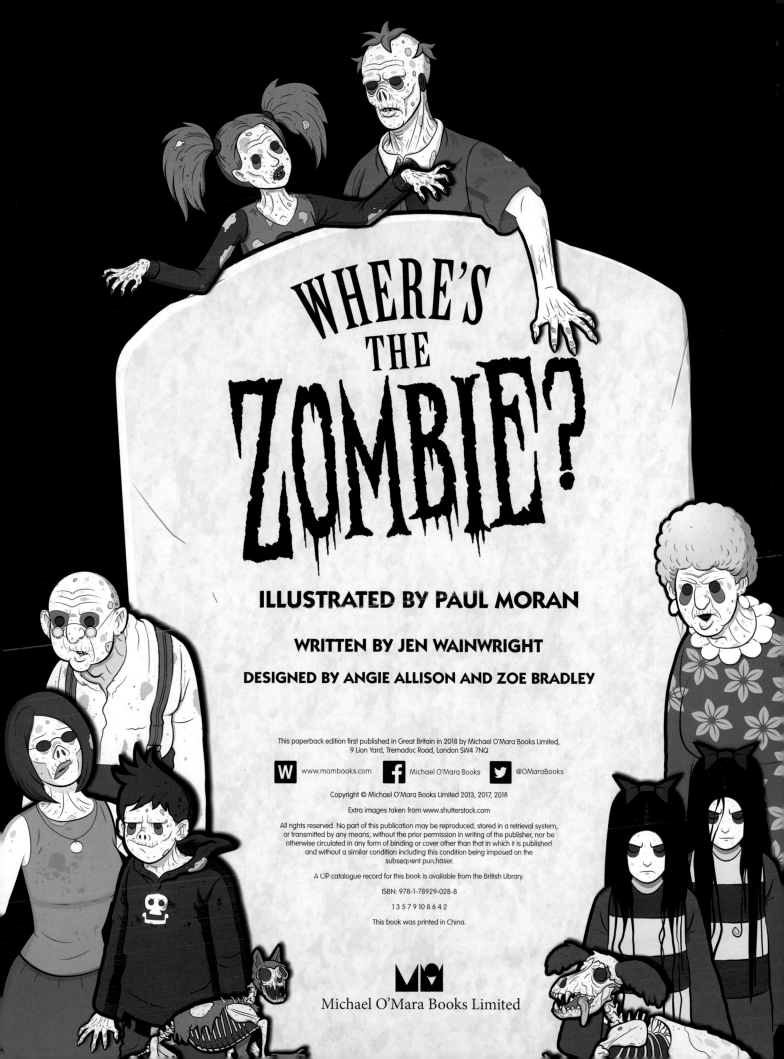

WHERE'S THE ZOMBIE?

ILLUSTRATED BY PAUL MORAN

WRITTEN BY JEN WAINWRIGHT

DESIGNED BY ANGIE ALLISON AND ZOE BRADLEY

This paperback edition first published in Great Britain in 2018 by Michael O'Mara Books Limited,
9 Lion Yard, Tremadoc Road, London SW4 7NQ

W www.mombooks.com   f Michael O'Mara Books   🐦 @OMaraBooks

Copyright © Michael O'Mara Books Limited 2013, 2017, 2018

Extra images taken from www.shutterstock.com

A CIP catalogue record for this book is available from the British Library.

ISBN: 978-1-78929-028-8

1 3 5 7 9 10 8 6 4 2

This book was printed in China.

Michael O'Mara Books Limited

OUTBREAK AT LABORATORY

FEBRUARY 11th

Scientist Joel Peters is being held under quarantine after an accident at Hart Laboratories, upstate New York, last week.

Peters, 42, appears to have been exposed to a highly concentrated strain of a new virus, code named ZX-5, which he was developing at the lab.

NAME: J PETERS
EMPLOYEE NO: 24576
CLEARANCE LEVEL: 2

THE PETERS FAMILY AT A SUMMER BARBECUE LAST YEAR

Peters is described by his colleagues as a hardworking and reliable man. 'We don't understand how this happened,' said a source at the lab. 'His work is always so meticulous.'

He was removed from the home he shares with his elderly parents, wife Martha and four children on Saturday.

The exact nature of his symptoms is unclear, but doctors report a marked deterioration in his condition in the last 24 hours. His family was unavailable for comment.

PETERS FAMILY ON THE RUN

FEBRUARY 20th

Central News can reveal that Joel Peters has escaped from the secure quarantine unit where he was being held. It was confirmed yesterday that his family and pets are also infected with virus ZX-5. They have been reported missing.

Images of the Peters family have been released nationwide. Citizens are urged not to approach them under any circumstances.

'It is vital that the Peters family are located and safely contained,' said the head of Hart Laboratories last night.

'Please be on the lookout for them, and report any sightings to the police immediately. We urgently need to study them to understand more about how this extremely unpredictable virus operates.'

● REC   10:23:32

WARNING: DO NOT APPROACH THESE PEOPLE OR THESE ANIMALS. THEY ARE HIGHLY CONTAGIOUS AND EXTREMELY DANGEROUS.

Search for the ten members of the missing Peters family on every page. There are also ten medical kits to spot on each page to aid those thought to be infected.

BREAKING NEWS: March 3rd

City hospital quarantined after outbreak of new virus.

Baffled doctors describe victims as 'walking dead'.

Have you seen this family?

LIVE

BREAKING NEWS: March 8th

Officials concerned virus may be airborne.

Citizens strongly advised to avoid crowded public spaces.

Have you seen this family?

LIVE

ZUCCX

BREAKING NEWS: March 17th

Infection is spreading at speed in urban areas.

Officials now classifying the virus as a Level 1 epidemic.

Have you seen this family?

BREAKING NEWS: March 22nd

Schools across the region to close.

Ringhill High remaining open despite fears.

Have you seen this family?

BREAKING NEWS: March 30th

Families transform subway station into bunker.

Panic sets in as number of infected victims keeps rising.

Have you seen this family?

LIVE

BREAKING NEWS: March 31st

Looters target city's banking district.

Armed thieves ignore high risk of contamination from infected 'zombies'.

Have you seen this family?

LIVE

BREAKING NEWS: April 4th

Confirmed zombie sightings outside urban exclusion zones.

Crisis talks are being held as containment efforts fail.

Have you seen this family?

BREAKING NEWS: April 10th

White House overrun.

President evacuated to safe house in the face of zombie riots.

Have you seen this family?

LIVE

BREAKING NEWS: April 16th

Panlc buying begins as groceries are depleted.

Violence erupts at superstore after food supplies run low.

Have you seen this family?

LIVE

BREAKING NEWS: April 22nd

Chaos on the roads.

Survivors head for ports in huge numbers.

Have you seen this family?

LIVE

BREAKING NEWS: April 28th

Saharan plane crash tragedy.

All crash survivors confirmed as infected.

Have you seen this family?

BREAKING NEWS: April 30th

Bands of vigilantes vow to stand and fight.

Battle in the streets as groups of brave survivors arm themselves against zombies.

Have you seen this family?

LIVE

BREAKING NEWS: May 2nd

Military drafted in to help worst hit areas.

Relief as helicopters arrive bringing supplies and weapons.

Have you seen this family?

LIVE

BREAKING NEWS: May 5th

Underground evacuation plan aborted.

Zombies attack Silvertown sewers, blocking planned escape route.

LIVE

Have you seen this family?

BREAKING NEWS: May 6th

Attack on Lightning Science Laboratories.

Zombie raid destroys prototype antidote.

Have you seen this family?

LIVE

BREAKING NEWS: May 9th

Zombie "nest" discovered near stronghold.

Elimination forces sent in urgently to cleanse the area.

Have you seen this family?

LIVE

BREAKING NEWS: May 12th

Strongholds X and Y breached.

Survivors flee to Fortress Z, the only remaining stronghold.

Have you seen this family?

LIVE

BREAKING NEWS: May 15th

Fortress Z falls …

Answers

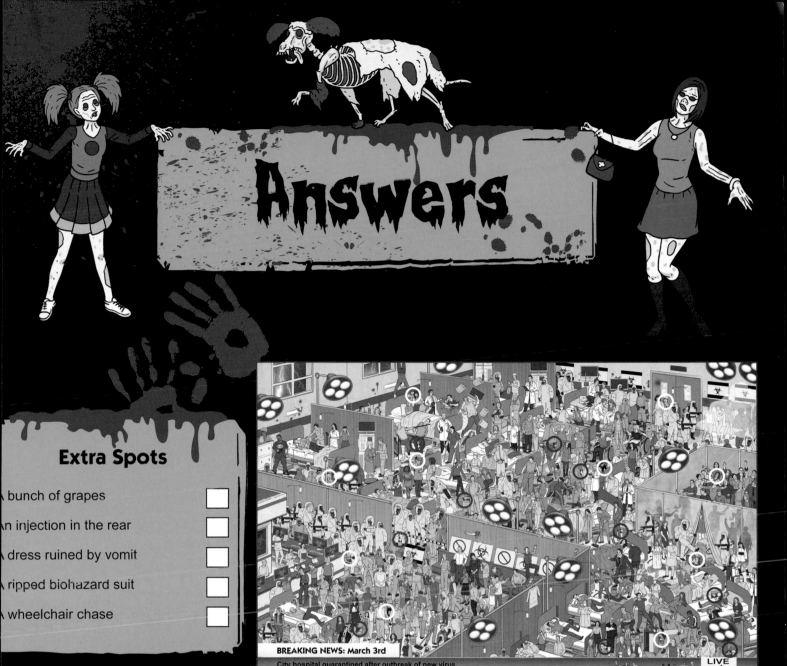

Extra Spots

- A bunch of grapes
- An injection in the rear
- A dress ruined by vomit
- A ripped biohazard suit
- A wheelchair chase

BREAKING NEWS: March 3rd
City hospital quarantined after outbreak of new virus.
Baffled doctors describe victims as 'walking dead'   Have you seen this family?

LIVE

BREAKING NEWS: March 8th
Officials concerned virus may be airborne.
Citizens strongly advised to avoid crowded public spaces.   Have you seen this family?

LIVE

Extra Spots

- A grinning clown
- A gruesome catch of the day
- A zombie police officer
- Eight rabbits
- A romantic carriage ride

BREAKING NEWS: March 17th

Infection is spreading at speed in urban areas.
Officials now classifying the virus as a Level 1 epidemic.

Have you seen this family?

LIVE

Extra Spots

A 'shop dummy' gone wild

A giant dog losing his head

An attack with a handbag

A feisty grandma with an umbrella

Two red shopping bags

Extra Spots

A zombie and a human kissing

Nine bananas

A zombie hand in a bag

A geek with a briefcase

A wedgie

BREAKING NEWS: March 22nd

Schools across the region to close.
Ringhill High remaining open despite fears.

Have you seen this family?

LIVE

BREAKING NEWS: March 30th

Families transform subway station into bunker.
Panic sets in as number of infected victims keeps rising.

Have you seen this family?

LIVE

Extra Spots

A man with a voodoo doll

A kettle being used as a weapon

Three priests

A man with an eye patch

A zombie with underpants on his face

BREAKING NEWS: March 31st
Looters target city's banking district.
Armed thieves ignore high risk of contamination from infected 'zombies'. Have you seen this family?

LIVE

BREAKING NEWS: April 4th
Confirmed zombie sightings outside urban exclusion zone.
Crisis talks are being held as containment efforts fail. Have you seen this family?

LIVE

BREAKING NEWS: April 10th
White House overrun.
President evacuated to safe house in the face of zombie riots. Have you seen this family?

LIVE

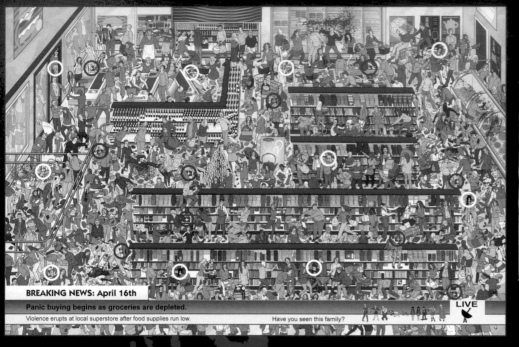

Extra Spots

A really heavy backpack

A lawnmower attack

A zombie hiding in a display

A zombie with a pineapple

A dramatic high kick

Extra Spots

A zombie chef

A grandma with a pistol

A man being dragged from his car

A gruesome pom pom

A zombie on a skateboard

Extra Spots

A zombie in a Hawaiian shirt

Three swimming pool inflatables

A drinks trolley

A suitcase with stamps on it

A teddy bear with one leg

Extra Spots

A lit stick of dynamite ☐

A powerful punch to the head ☐

Steak as bait ☐

A delicious green brain ☐

A zombie with an arrow through her head ☐

BREAKING NEWS: April 30th
Band of vigilantes vow to stand and fight.
Battle in the streets as groups of brave survivors arm themselves against zombies.   Have you seen this family?   LIVE

Extra Spots

...lands being sliced off ☐

...sliding tackle ☐

...burst water tank ☐

...man in a top hat ☐

...woman with a tattoo ☐

BREAKING NEWS: May 2nd
Military drafted in to help worst hit areas.
Relief as helicopters arrive bringing supplies and weapons.   Have you seen this family?   LIVE

Extra Spots

Eight alligators ☐

A roll of pink toilet paper ☐

A power drill to the knee ☐

A pick axe through the face ☐

A rat attack ☐

BREAKING NEWS: May 5th
Underground evacuation plan aborted.
Zombies attack Silvertown sewers, blocking planned escape route.   Have you seen this family?   LIVE

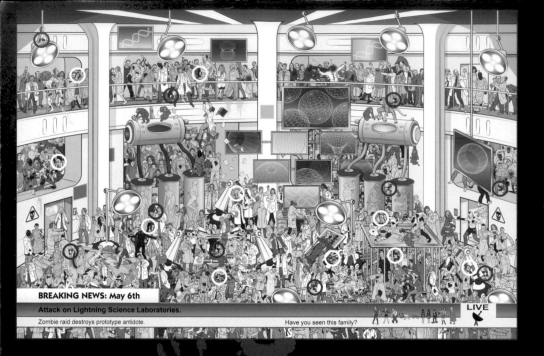

BREAKING NEWS: May 6th

Attack on Lightning Science Laboratories.

Zombie raid destroys prototype antidote.

Have you seen this family?

LIVE

Extra Spots

A monkey with a gross plaything ☐

A laptop in midair ☐

A zombie with a cow's head ☐

A mutant dog peeing ☐

Attack of the killer slime ☐

Extra Spots

A zombie superhero ☐

A dog going for the privates ☐

A decaying cow's head ☐

A soldier dodging a zombie bullet ☐

One bright red stiletto heel ☐

BREAKING NEWS: May 9th

Zombie "nest" discovered near stronghold.

Elimination forces sent in urgently to cleanse the area.

Have you seen this family?

LIVE

BREAKING NEWS: May 12th

Strongholds X and Y breached.

Survivors flee to Fortress Z, the only remaining stronghold.

Have you seen this family?

LIVE

Extra Spots

A vulture's dinner ☐

A woman in a surgical mask ☐

Three exposed brains ☐

An explosion ☐

A pilot in trouble ☐